P9-DMI-579

Pitch and Throw, Grasp and Know

What Is a Synonym?

To my brother Danny—
the wordsmith of the family
—B.P.C.

Pitch and Throw, Grasp and Know

What Is a Synonym?

by Brian P. Cleary

illustrated by Brian Gable

CAROLRHODA BOOKS, INC. / MINNEAPOLIS

Do you feel **tired** or **beat** or **exhausted**

from making the cake
that you've baked
and you've frosted?

Because there are **SYNONYMS**, you get to choose

Synonyms
help us be
less repetitious

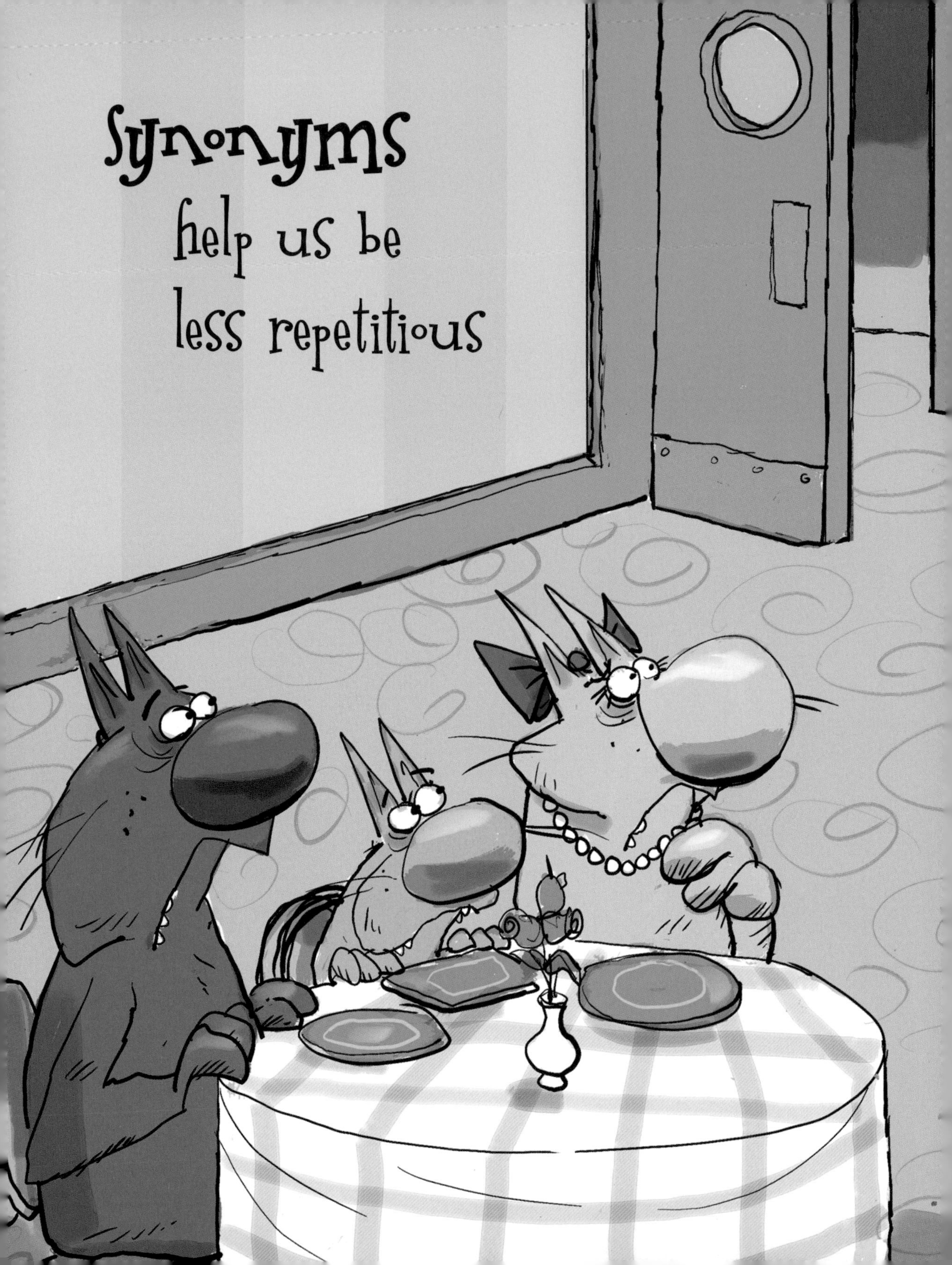

by letting us choose
between blue plates or dishes.

They give us
more options
and make things
precise,

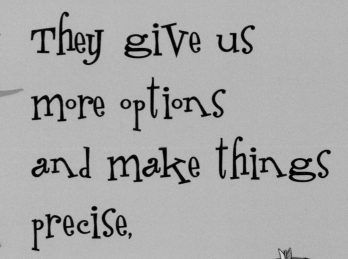

comprehend
and grasp
and know.

Richness and depth
are what synonyms raise

When they're used in
a paragraph, sentence, or phrase.

A lovely and pretty and beautiful city.

Cat
Feline
Kitty

A cat
or a feline
could be called a kitty.

They let us pick showering, raining, or pouring.

Without them,
our language would
surely be boring!

for the sneakers
or tennis shoes,

yellow or golden.

Don't you agree
that it's pretty appealing,

We have all these choices
to say how we're feeling?

ABOUT THE AUTHOR & ILLUSTRATOR

BRIAN P. CLEARY is the author of the Words Are Categorical series, including A Mink, a Fink, a Skating Rink: What Is a Noun? and Hairy, Scary, Ordinary: What Is an Adjective?, and of Rainbow Soup: Adventures in Poetry. He lives in Cleveland, Ohio.

BRIAN GABLE is the illustrator of Dearly, Nearly, Insincerely: What Is an Adverb? and the Make Me Laugh joke books. He lives in Toronto, Ontario, with his wife and two children.

Text copyright © 2005 by Brian P. Cleary
Illustrations copyright © 2005 by Brian Gable

Carolrhoda Books, Inc.,
A division of Lerner Publishing Group
241 First Avenue North
Minneapolis, MN 55401 U.S.A.

Website address: www.carolrhodabooks.com

Library of Congress Cataloging-in-Publication Data

Cleary, Brian P., 1959-
    Pitch and throw, grasp and know : what is a synonym? / by Brian P. Cleary;
illustrated by Brian Gable.
       p.   cm. — (Words are categorical)
    ISBN: 1-57505-796-4 (lib. bdg. : alk. paper)
    1. English language—Synonyms and antonyms—Juvenile literature. I. Gable,
Brian, 1949- II. Title. III. Series.
PE1591.C56 2005
    428.1—dc22   2004011975

Manufactured in the United States of America
1 2 3 4 5 6 — JR — 10 09 08 07 06 05